Sun

High Output Management

by Andrew S. Grove

Instaread

Please Note

This is a summary with analysis.

Table of Contents

Overview

First published in 1983, *High Output Management* by Andrew Grove is a management guide based on Grove's 15 years of managerial experience and knowledge as a co-founder, president, and chief executive of Intel. As Grove emphasizes in a new introduction to the book, globalization and the information revolution have dramatically changed the workforce, making people ever more replaceable and the market ever more competitive. Companies must adapt to these changes or face their own irrelevance and extinction. The same holds true for workers and managers. Managers, especially middle managers, are often overlooked in business books and forgotten in organizations, yet they are immensely important not only to businesses but to society more broadly. In order to survive and to thrive in their careers, managers must constantly enhance their value by learning and adapting to a changing, often unpredictable business environment.

By applying methods to production, exercising managerial leverage, and eliciting a desire for peak performance, managers of all types — lawyers, engineers, teachers, accountants, consultants, and general middle managers —

can work more productively. Ultimately, managers should measure their value in the output of the organization for which they work. Managers should therefore spend their time increasing the output of value of the people they supervise. That is, managers enhance their value as employees by enhancing the output of their subordinates and associates, not simply themselves. In a competitive, evolving marketplace, there is no point at which the work of adding value should stop. Rather, the key to survival for managers is to be constantly searching for new ways to add value and maintain a competitive advantage.

This is the third edition of this now-classic management book.

Important People

Andrew "Andy" Grove (born András István Gróf) is an American businessman and a founder of Intel who has served as the company's president and chief executive officer. The author of several books on business and manufacturing, Grove taught at the Stanford University Graduate School of Business for 24 years.

Ben Horowitz is an American businessman, technology entrepreneur, and the co-founder of the venture capital firm Andreessen Horowitz. He is the author of *The Hard Thing About Hard Things: Building a Business When There Are No Easy Answers* (2014) and also wrote the foreword to the latest edition of *High Output Management* (2015).

Key Takeaways

1. In the modern, globalized business environment, everything happens faster. The information revolution means that knowledge spreads to more people much more quickly than it once did.

2. The modern workplace has become much more competitive and much less kind. Everyone is ultimately replaceable, and people must learn to enhance their value constantly to maintain an advantage.

3. Due to the fast pace of change, the business world has also become less predictable. Managers must be mentally and emotionally comfortable with chaos and learn to anticipate the unexpected.

4. Managers should think about management in terms of what they produce, and apply the principles of manufacturing to how they go about supervising and motivating employees.

5. A manager's output consists of the output of all the people being supervised. High managerial productivity depends on focusing on tasks that will have the greatest impact on a team's output.

6. To run an operation successfully and measure impact, managers need to use a set of indicators. Each indicator should focus on a specific operational goal.

7. A team only performs as well as the individuals in it. Managers should try to elicit team members' peak performance.

8. Changes in the work environment today have altered the relationships between managers and their subordinates. Managers must adapt to these changes in the way they manage and communicate with subordinates and associates.

Thank you for purchasing this Instaread book

**Download the Instaread mobile app to get
unlimited text & audio summaries
of bestselling books.**

Visit Instaread.co
to learn more.

Analysis

Key Takeaway 1

In the modern, globalized business environment, everything happens faster. The information revolution means that knowledge spreads to more people much more quickly than it once did.

Analysis

Email is the most obvious example of dramatic changes in information flow and management. With the same effort that it once took to reach one person, a manager can now reach many people at the same time, spreading necessary knowledge much more rapidly and broadly than was once possible.

But there is a downside to this rapid increase in speed. Email can divide workers' attention, interrupting their workflow with constant new questions and demands on their time. Intra-office communication systems, like Slack, pose a very similar problem. They also set the expectation that workers should be able to respond to email or other instant communications around the clock. But studies show that this actually doesn't improve output. In fact, such expectations can do more harm than good. [1]

The need to constantly stay on top of things, to anticipate sudden changes or curveballs, is part and parcel of surviving in the modern business environment. The reality is that it is also making life more stressful: people never really get a break from work, they're never really off the clock or on vacation. Instead, the new normal is to be constantly "checked in" to the office, with little respite.

Key Takeaway 2

The modern workplace has become much more competitive and much less kind. Everyone is ultimately replaceable, and people must learn to enhance their value constantly to maintain an advantage.

Analysis

The fast pace of the business environment and surfeit of eager workers means there is almost always someone angling to replace any individual. Managers must dedicate themselves to creating new value by staying vitally connected to their companies and industries: they must remain informed about the latest changes in technology and techniques, and ensure that they aren't merely passing along information but actually making things better for their organizations.

The extreme competitiveness of today's work environment, and the need for managers to carefully manage their own careers while fending off threats, creates considerable anxiety around building and maintaining a rewarding career. This manifests in the huge industry of career management advice, like Buzzfeed lists of the top habits of successful people and *Harvard Business Review* studies of best management practices.

Part of this increased atmosphere of competitiveness stems from transformations in the global economy, including mechanization, offshoring, and stagnant wages, which have made jobs more precarious and heightened the demands for "lean" management. The Population Reference Bureau noted in 2008 that though the offshoring of manufacturing jobs has been occurring for decades, the offshoring of service sector jobs is a fairly new phenomenon, and the numbers of jobs moving overseas was rising rapidly. [2] It is estimated that one-fifth of the US workforce is vulnerable to offshoring. A Global Research study of offshoring drew particularly alarmist conclusions regarding the phenomenon, calling offshoring a greater threat to American society than terrorism. [3]

Key Takeaway 3

Due to the fast pace of change, the business world has also become less predictable. Managers must be mentally and emotionally comfortable with chaos and learn to anticipate the unexpected.

Analysis

Being a manager today requires an ability to handle chaos. Managers should try to foresee changes in their industries by staying abreast of the latest developments and technology, but they also have to be prepared for sudden, unforeseeable changes and be skilled at adapting quickly to whatever is thrown their way.

It is by now a commonplace to describe the early twenty-first century as an age of business innovation and technological disruption, with new techniques, startups, apps, and technologies transforming the way long-standing businesses and industries operate. Ride-sharing businesses such as Uber and Lyft have disrupted the taxi industry. E-book readers and digital subscriptions seemed, for a time, to threaten traditional forms of reading, such as newspapers and magazines. Meanwhile, the financial crisis of 2008 severely damaged numerous industries, causing people in a wide range of careers, including banking, law, and journalism, to lose their jobs. For instance, advertising revenue for newspapers plummeted as a result of the economic downturn. Between 2008 and 2010, eight major newspaper chains declared bankruptcy, city papers shut down, and many laid off reporters and editors, reduced salaries, and even stopped producing print publications. [4]

But as many business leaders have pointed out, sudden changes and challenges don't always have to be interpreted as a bad thing. In fact, problems can also be opportunities, a chance to grow a career or a company by finding ways to adapt, evolve, and address a new twist. Journalism still hasn't fully recovered, but many publications have started experimenting successfully with other ways to bring in revenue and reach readers. Some have introduced paywalls, for instance, and many are pursuing digital and social media strategies.

Key Takeaway 4

Managers should think about management in terms of what they produce, and apply the principles of manufacturing to how they go about supervising and motivating employees.

Analysis

A manufacturing approach to management means creating and delivering products for customers according to established expectations for time, quality, and cost. Everyone is a manufacturer or producer in some sense, and it is helpful to think about managerial work as overseeing a production line. For instance, even in the ride-sharing industry, which does not produce a physical product for sale, managers might still think about the most effective way to match riders with cars, how to ensure that cars pick up riders in a timely fashion, how to guarantee the quality and safety of the ride, and the cost at which they can both draw riders and still continue to turn a profit.

This efficiency model for thinking about business can be applied to any number of industries and management goals. New environmentally friendly industries have been interested, for instance, in reducing congestion, pollution, and parking problems. This has resulted in a rise in biking and ride-sharing companies. Data shows that by streamlining the way people commute around a city, congestion and pollution can be reduced. [5]

Key Takeaway 5

A manager's output consists of the output of all the people being supervised. High managerial productivity depends on focusing on tasks that will have the greatest impact on a team's output.

Analysis

In some sense, it is difficult to measure a manager's success or output; it is not as straightforward as measuring the number of products made or sold. Managers do not always oversee production lines or direct sales output, but the people they manage do. Thus, their output can be measured in the output of the people they manage.

Take the example of Cutco, for instance, which is a company that sells cutlery and other kitchen items. Cutco relies in large part on individual salespeople, whose output can be calculated in terms of the number of knife sets they are able to sell to customers. Cutco's managers oversee salespeople, and their own success can, in a sense, be measured in terms of the success and output of the sales team. This is to say that a Cutco manager is productive when he or she does a good job of training staff about the products, motivating them to make sales, coaching them through slumps or frustrations, and making sure they feel satisfied and excited in their jobs. A good manager would constantly look for ways in which the sales team's output can be improved and he or she can help them deliver more value for the company. One aspect of this work is communication: ensuring team members have all the information and support they need to perform at their best.

Key Takeaway 6

To run an operation successfully and measure impact, managers need to use a set of indicators. Each indicator should focus on a specific operational goal.

Analysis

For a traditional factory, impact indicators might involve such tools as a sales forecast, a material inventory, an updated knowledge of the condition of equipment, an assessment of the required manpower, and finally, a way to gauge quality.

Managers must customize this general template of indicators according to the specific operational goals of their company and of the people they oversee. Thus, these indicators would probably look different for different industries and companies. A manager of Cutco employees would have to design indicators that respond to the specific tasks and goals of the cutlery sales business. Thus, a sales forecast might assess how many people are potentially interested in buying new knife and utensil sets. A material inventory would look at how many products are available to sell and how many more need to be manufactured to meet sales projections. Similarly, where manpower is concerned, a manager should determine how many salespeople are required in major cities and regions to meet sales expectations and turn the profit that managers hope to reach. In addition to salespeople, managers

need to think about other important personnel, like labor-
ers at Cutco factories and receptionists and administrators
at Cutco offices. Finally, there's the question of quality:
how to gauge whether customers are satisfied with their
Cutco knives. The rise or fall of sales might be one indicator of this: People who like their knives are likely to spread
the word about how great the product is, which would
encourage more people to open their doors to salespeople and consider buying their own Cutco knives. Online
reviews and other customer ratings systems are also useful
ways to gauge customer satisfaction with the quality of
the products.

Key Takeaway 7

A team only performs as well as the individuals in it. Managers should try to elicit team members' peak performance.

Analysis

"Peak performance" and "personal best" are terms most frequently heard in the sports world. But they are also useful analogies for business managers to use when considering how to encourage employees to work at their highest level and perform well for the company. When lots of people achieve their personal bests, teams and businesses as a whole succeed.

The question of how to ensure that the people a manager supervises reach for their peak performances is a bit more tricky, especially because different people might be motivated by different things and in different ways. This is where a manager's relationship with employees becomes especially important: Managers must establish a rapport and understand what motivates specific people and why, under what conditions they perform best, and what they as managers can do to solicit better work output. In some instances, the answer might be simple: People are motivated by a paycheck and the possibility of a promotion or other financial incentive. But for many workers, money alone is not sufficient as a motivator. Psychological research has shown that people often do their best work because it is work they love, or because it advances a goal they care passionately about, or because the work is done in collaboration with people who they finding energizing and inspiring. [6] By spending time with employees both in formal settings like meetings and conferences, and in more casual, social venues, managers can better understand what will help people reach their personal best. This information can be invaluable for constructing a team in which people are satisfied with their roles, functions, and relationships with their co-workers.

Key Takeaway 8

Changes in the work environment today have altered the relationships between managers and their subordinates. Managers must adapt to these changes in the way they manage and communicate with subordinates and associates.

Analysis

The use of email as an efficient way of communicating with a large group of people is, in many ways, a beneficial tool for managing in the twenty-first century. But there are also ways in which email can alter work relationships and management styles for the worse. For instance, it is not necessarily a good thing that managers do not need to meet and speak with their employees as frequently. Email, especially group or mass emails, isn't always a decent substitute for in-person, one-on-one conversation.

Depersonalized communication makes the business environment ever more impersonal, with employees spending much of their time engaged with a glass screen. One of the possible accompanying risks is that employees might become dissatisfied with their work environments and unmotivated by relationships that exist primarily through electronic interfaces. They also might feel less loyalty to the company they work for, fewer commitments to the co-workers and managers they communicate with, and less interest in helping the business reach its best output. A Forbes survey shows that poor communication is one of the key reasons for employee dissatisfaction. Workers who don't have positive office friendships don't like going to the office; by contrast, friendships with co-workers can make work much more enjoyable, but it's hard to build these friendships in environments where workers are increasingly isolated. [7] The benefits of more efficient, streamlined modes of communication should be weighed against these drawbacks and the long-term effects they could have on worker and company success.

Author's Style

Grove divides his book into four parts: The Breakfast Factory, Management Is a Team Game, Team of Teams, and The Players. Each part is broken down into several chapters. Though Grove's book is aimed at managers, especially middle managers, his ideas about adding value, leveraging performance, and adapting in an ever-changing, competitive environment are applicable to readers from a wide range of industries.

Grove makes frequent use of business terminology and lingo, such as production flow, output, indicators, and so forth. Nevertheless, his language is accessible to lay readers unfamiliar with the ins and outs of management. In addition to the management and industry examples, he also uses more everyday examples to describe his principles. The "breakfast factory" and the sports analogy of "peak performance" are two such examples, and these analogies are what help make his points accessible to readers who are less familiar with the business world.

In addition to numerous examples and anecdotal descriptions, Grove relies on charts, diagrams, and graphs to illustrate his management principles. These are useful in making some of his abstract suggestions more vivid and concrete, especially for readers new to management texts. Additionally, Grove has updated his book with an introduction that takes into account significant changes in business since the book's original publication in 1983. This introduction provides a useful update for twenty-first century readers, orienting them to the most relevant problems in the modern workforce. At the same time, it maintains that the original management principles he set down are still useful for meeting these challenges.

Author's Perspective

Grove's book is based on his 15 years of managerial experience at Intel, which he joined at its inception in 1968. He is eager to impart this knowledge to a wide range of readers in a broad swath of industries, but he aims his book particularly at middle managers, whom he considers to be the important but often overlooked members of organizations. In this updated edition, there is an urgent tone to Grove's message about the principles of management because he recognizes that everyone is replaceable and that the forces of globalization have been tremendously destabilizing for many people's careers. Writing from this perspective and understanding, he hopes to help people compete more successfully in the modern workforce.

~~~~ END OF INSTAREAD ~~~~

Thank you for purchasing this Instaread book

**Download the Instaread mobile app to get
unlimited text & audio summaries
of bestselling books.**

Visit Instaread.co
to learn more.

References

1. Thomas, Maura. "Your Late-Night Emails Are Hurting Your Team." *Harvard Business Review.* March 16, 2015. Accessed February 25, 2016. https://hbr.org/2015/03/your-late-night-emails-are-hurting-your-team

2. Hira, Ron. "Offshoring U.S. Labor Increasing." Population Reference Bureau. 2008. Accessed February 25, 2016.

3. http://www.prb.org/Publications/Articles/2008/offshoring.aspx

4. Roberts, Paul Craig. "The Offshoring of American Jobs: A Greater Threat Than Terrorism." Global Research. Centre for Research on Globalization. February 2010. Accessed February 25, 2016. http://www.globalresearch.ca/the-offshore-outsourcing-of-american-jobs-a-greater-threat-than-terrorism/18725

5. Kirchoff, Suzanne M. "The U.S. Newspaper Industry in Transition." Congressional Research Service. September 9, 2010. Accessed February 25, 2016. https://www.fas.org/sgp/crs/misc/R40700.pdf

6. "New data reveals the obvious: Car sharing cuts congestion, pollution." *The Maylay Mail Online.* July 17, 2015. Accessed February 25,

2016. http://www.themalaymailonline.com/drive/article/car-sharing-effective-in-reducing-in-congestion-pollution

7. Pink, Daniel. *Drive: The Surprising Truth About What Motivates Us.* New York: Riverhead, 2011.

8. Hedges, Kristi. "8 Common Causes Of Workplace Demotivation." *Forbes.* January 20, 2014. Accessed February 25, 2016. http://www.forbes.com/sites/work-in-progress/2014/01/20/8-common-causes-of-workplace-demotivation/2/#36cefb7af401